praise for Almo

I n this collection of deeply, intimate conversations, addresses, and meditations, Jennifer Wallace follows the most fearsome states of being into realms of tender beauty. In her sight, nothing is to be turned away from—not the granite of human loneliness, the unexpectedly bright hues of loss, the vitality of grief, or the sharp challenges born of authentic spiritual striving. Wallace's eye and heart roam freely among the mysteries (without, as Keats wrote, any "irritable reaching after fact or reason") and in roaming, find that abundant field where we might touch again "those whose light made us more visible."

—LIA PURPURA, author of *It Shouldn't Have Been Beautiful*

J ennifer Wallace writes, "I have a softness in me that I want / to be closer to." These poems, one after the next, labor toward something like that softness— laboring which is not only elegant, but clumsy and craving and scared and utterly human. Which makes this book a good guide, a good companion, toward our own softness. To which I, too, more than just about anything, want to be closer.

—ROSS GAY, author of *Catalog of Unabashed Gratitude*

I n poem after poem, Jennifer Wallace strives to capture the experience of being alive in the context of particular experiences in which she both memorializes and praises at the same time. Admirably comfortable with deceptively quotidian subject matter, no matter how small or seemingly negligible, Wallace conjures shining details that convey the deeply evocative pathos of ordinary things through the lens of memory and perspicacity. Indeed, her poems appear to come to her—in John Keats's phrase—"as naturally as leaves to a tree."

In her poem "Miracle," Wallace writes her own memorable *ars poetica* with admirable balance between telling and showing: "Miracle means also: / not to shy away from, but to become / awesome, like light through the branches / ushering into existence / each tip of insignificant grass." These are refreshingly mature lyrical poems reminding us of who we are anew in our most familiar settings.

—CHARD DENIORD, Vermont Poet Laureate

The poet walks me from one pause to another and yet another. In the pauses, picture-phrases and lean, clear emotions lift me and set me down, sing to me and fall silent. What a lovely walk. And how lightly does the wisdom rest on me and wait for my recognition. Wallace helps us identify what the soul has already learned.

—VINITA HAMPTON WRIGHT,
author of *The St. Teresa of Avila Prayer Book*

Religious or spiritual writing tends to fall into the trap of being either willfully obscure, or too quickly cutting to "God" as the general answer to all particular vexations. In the religious poems in this collection, Wallace strikes a lovely balance. With no attempt to tame or pin down the divine, she names with confidence where God is, or well could be, in this world. Her poems wade into the shadows of life, without being proud of their own gloom. They are unafraid to be wise; to not only describe reality but make wise assertions about what life does to us.

Here, Catholic images are rendered fresh. Candles blessing a throat on the Memorial of St. Blaise unspool into an image where, "It might take another 50 years until something triggers the silky comfort against our throats . . . the scissor-shaped pressure."

"We know the number of the gene / but not the day the strand will break." Lines like this make short work of the native human condition: awe at our stunning progress, at all we have come to know, and an even deeper awe at what we ultimately cannot know.

The lines ring with simple and pitch perfect phrasing: "Tell me, someone: / with the spade of days remaining, / how to turn the soil / and where." These lines are accessible, but not in a way where "accessible" is code for: there's not much going on here. It means rather the words are put together in a way that makes you want to get to the end of the poem and see just what this author is up to. In short, they are compelling.

—BR. JOE HOOVER, SJ, poetry editor at *America Magazine*

Jennifer Wallace's poems, clear and measured in their language, while incandescent in their vision, show what happens when the ordinary is ennobled: we are souls, rather than mere selves, and the world we inhabit, while prey to tragedy and indifference at every turn, is still a world fit for wonder and grace. This is a marvelous work that stands with Cairns and Oliver, Wiman and Glück, reclaiming the sacred in the steady rumor of its eclipse.

—DAVID RIGSBEE, author of *Not Alone in My Dancing: Essays and Reviews*

p o e m s

Almost
Entirely

JENNIFER WALLACE

PARACLETE PRESS
BREWSTER, MASSACHUSETTS

2017 First Printing

Almost Entirely: Poems

Copyright © 2017 by Jennifer Wallace

ISBN 978-1-61261-859-3

Stand By Me, Words and Music by Jerry Leiber, Mike Stoller and Ben E. King
Copyright (c) 1961 Sony/ATV Music Publishing LLC, Copyright Renewed
All Rights Administered by Sony/ATV Music Publishing LLC, 424 Church Street, Suite
1200, Nashville, TN, 37219
International Copyright Secured All Rights Reserved
Reprinted by Permission of Hal Leonard LLC

The Paraclete Press name and logo (dove on cross) are trademarks of Paraclete
Press, Inc.

Library of Congress Cataloging-in-Publication Data
Names: Wallace, Jennifer, 1954- author.
Title: Almost entirely : poems / Jennifer Wallace.
Description: Brewster, Massachusetts : Paraclete Press Inc., [2017]
Identifiers: LCCN 2017036835 | ISBN 9781612618593 (softcover)
Classification: LCC PS3573.A4263 A6 2017 | DDC 811/.54—dc23
LC record available at https://lccn.loc.gov/   2017036835

10 9 8 7 6 5 4 3 2 1

Published by Paraclete Press
Brewster, Massachusetts
www.paracletepress.com

Printed in the United States of America

It sure is hard work: governing
my Western mind. Faith/Reason. Reason/
Faith. Borges said, "The writer
must not destroy by human reasonings
the faith that art requires of us."

CONTENTS

Carruth / 11
when the wing gives way / 13

When The Wing Gives Way / 15
And God Goes Blank / 16
Doubt / 17
Thamar Dreamt Of Birds In Her Throat / 18
The Problem Of Attending / 19
The Wind Of God / 20
Requiem / 21
Atonement / 26
Branch, Drop / 27
Nothing Is Too Wonderful To Be True / 28
Triton / 29
Learning How To Pray / 30

something for us to stand on / 31

We Know How It Works / 33
Life's Second Half / 34
Reliable Equation / 35
Dream / 36
Each Life Opens / 37
Going Without Tea / 38
At Daybreak, Waiting For The Oriole Under The Serviceberry Tree / 39
Urine Of Cows Fed On Mango Leaves / 40

This Evening / 41

I Am Not Persian / 42

Friendship / 43

I Don't Like People; Animals, Too, Are An Imposition / 44

Radio / 45

I Have A Softness In Me / 46

The Idealist / 47

The Inner Place Of Finding You / 48

Tumor / 49

Stand By Me / 50

Until Now / 51

Cul-de-sac / 52

Restless / 53

An Agreeable Burden / 54

What It Must Be Like / 55

Opening / 56

The Want Fire / 57

Quickening / 58

First Heat / 59

How To Say It / 60

Coming To Terms With It / 61

State Of Emergency / 62

The Work Of Art / 63

Two Pockets / 64

The Road / 65

Epithalamion, 45 Years Hence / 66

one hundred footsteps / 67

like light through the branches / 73

Miracle / 75
What Landscape Paints Itself In Me / 76
Just A Day / 77
An Eagle's Table / 78
Although It's Wasted Now / 79
Our Lake Is Heart-Shaped / 80
Bashō At The Plate: An Ephemeral / 81
How To Paint A Walking Mountain / 82
Harvest, Hatfield, Massachusetts / 84
Treasure / 85
Axis Mundi / 86
Wayfinding / 87
Hammerhead / 88
What Do You Think / 90
Having Arrived On The Other Side / 91
Her Good Hat / 92
Becoming / 93
Intimate Distance / 94
The New England Graveyard Under Snow / 95
Cityscape / 96
The Bird Artist / 97
First Walk / 98

Aubade / 99

Prayer / 100

Readiness / 101

Becoming An Impressionist / 102

NOTES / 105

ACKNOWLEDGMENTS / 107

ABOUT THE AUTHOR / 109

Carruth

Carruth, my first-loved poet, said
in his "Testament": Now I am
almost entirely love. He
imagined his ego's heaviness
sifting through the hourglass's narrowness
and settling on a gathering
cone of love below.

He didn't know, then —
that when I lift his book from the shelf,
the love he has become spills
like galaxies in my hands.

when the wing gives way

When The Wing Gives Way

I

How to feel his death? On the street.
The shots. My friend's scream.
One cracked the air, the other
pierced the thin veil. A usual evening
returning from somewhere
returned from many times before.

When I look for where to fix the broken city that I love,
the whole tower wobbles. What the government hasn't done.
What the gunmen's parents didn't do.
What? What I haven't done with my puny song?

And now: the sirens.
And now: the neighbors say, "Did he resist?"
And now: how can I live in this place or any place?
Can I live with myself — a part of his self, lying there,
a part of the selves who dropped him there.
All of us, under the wing that is no wing.

II

In my mind-voice, without knowing why
or from where it came, a whisper:

> "When the wing gives way . . ."
> "When the wing gives way . . ."

I want to be more ready than I am today.
Ready to let what is left lift me, draw me into meanings
that will shatter me more than this.

And God Goes Blank

Three times today
I thought of God:

first with a man who watched the sky turn black . . .
"Weird, sort of desperate," he said.

Next in a poem by Rosenberg:
infinite wing
and dark gargoyles under it.
But from your center
light breaks through you —
the creator's voice
in your midst
in the midst of the world.

A student in her thesis wrote
of "little tabernacles, hush harbors."
Slave women hung wet quilts and hid there
to muffle their spiritual song.

Master, no master.

Doubt

I look at it this way: either you exist or you don't. I don't think —
in your case — that there's an in-between, a "sort of" God. And the
point seems to be not to think about it or to reason about it. But
here's the thing: If I am to believe in what others say (these others
being agents of yours), then I was made by you in your image. And
since I am predisposed by nature to question everything, it would
seem you wanted it this way. That you are also "this way." That you
sewed into me a weak thread that you hoped would unravel . . .
setting me off-course with respect to you. It's an odd strategy. But
the same one who invented oxygen invented doubt and I guess
that sort of variety keeps things moving, which you are a fan of.
No doubt about that.

Thamar Dreamt Of Birds In Her Throat

But not everyone has the benefit of such dreams. For some of us, the bishops intervene. Each year in deep winter — though older, wrinkled — we walk again from the parish school to the church. The bishop waits behind the rail with his tall hat. The creamy robe scrapes the marble floor. He is rarely seen without his gloves. The local priests precede him with unmarked boxes, plain white candlesticks piled high. Those who aren't the first to kneel bear witness. Some of us disappear again, unblessed. It might take another 50 years until something triggers the silky comfort against our throats . . . the scissor-shaped pressure.
The beating of wings.

The Problem Of Attending

According to Kierkegaard,
Christianity is not a consolation
but a demand.

Excited to know this.
Call me crazy, hardship appeals.
I've been waiting for it.

A few days ago while walking,
something made itself known in me —

And now
the problem of attending it begins.

The Wind Of God

. . . moved over the face of the waters. And after reading this,
the awareness that, more than once,
God has turned my head in the right direction,
yet I haven't seen the gesture for what it is.

The world charges and is charged with a white-hot flame.
I might turn away, but each morning my head is turned for me
toward a crow's flight, squirrel passage, or a person
with whom I share an ever-present reaching toward.
I let myself be turned sometimes. Sometimes
I get into my car and drive away.

Today I picture God's hand cupped atop my head —
a quiet turning and then receding.
We are "fine" with each other. This god has all the time in the world.

Requiem

ETERNAL LIGHT

Where are they?
Those whose light made us more visible . . .

No one's footsteps. No merry whistle on the stairs.
The hand we reach for.

When we trudge back from the stony field
the world is strangely the same, except
for the rip on the couch where he sat,
a thinness on the curb where she played.
And the knocking of our dulled attention.

We draw a circle around where they were.
Faith flickers there.

DAY OF RECKONING

Pinned to the window,
we search for what they took with them:
our fathers' names, the eyes
in which we crouched and flourished.

We want to talk to the dead.
A hawk appears, we give it meaning.
"Come back," we ask the sea,
the overcast sky.

Daybreak doesn't come
and when it comes for us, it keeps coming:
the neighbor stoops to tie her toddler's shoe,
the dog with its one brown ear,
and the clouds. Answering, not answering.

DAY OF DOUBT

In the cathedral we sang
O Lamb of God. *Requiem
aeternam dona eis, Domine.*

These rhythms
in which we plead,
through which what-we-are-not pleads with us:
the comfortable psalm
the tower bell, bone-deep
the rope that holds until we need it.

The third day has passed.
I have forgotten his voice.
It has become all voices.
A father gone
and with him, all fathers.

O cordless bell,
where is the shepherd, the sheltering wing?
O Lamb of God . . .
declare yourself by something other than
this leaving, this taking away.

DAY OF FAITH

Most of us believe in something:
the garden, a star, the scrape
of the stone rolling back.

I want to believe in his still chest,
hands folded at last. The stillness
we dreamt of. This man we knew,
now complex.

What is death but the truth of incompleteness?
An unpicked pear mottles in the grass.
The well fills and unfills.
One early sparrow can't help but sing.

OFFERING

In the beginning —

before the act
before Eden
before we named ourselves Desire
(wanting, not wanting)
and a raven flew from that place —

we claimed our inheritance:
landless, unequivocal

The nothingness that is not God.

Deliver us to our creation: this afterlife.
We'll make our offering: a collection of broken hours,
                    the urge to speak.

Deliver Them

Yellowed by the sun,
the once-woeful field shines with time.
A north wind clips the tiny grasses
but we deny the season, keeping
the last butterfly in view. It wants to fly.

We know better than to tether what we love.
Our cup of shadow overflowing.

The blue azure whispers up
and merges with the sky.
Up ahead: the sun-drenched track, greed-free,
from which the wing departs
and the new blade emerges.

Teach us to unbolt the door.

Eternal Rest

We draw a circle around where they were.
Faith flickers there.

Perhaps we are here to free the sparks
from grief's too small box, to light the way
for You who planted death within us so deeply
for You who chafe against our dark.

We come from the unknown and return there believing —

> The spinning earth, still as a deep lake.
> The fallen tree whose log crumbles,
> seed safely hidden in the clay.

— restless until we rest.

Perhaps we are here to make of earth a minor heaven
where birds will glide higher
in an air made more full
by the dead's barely audible sigh.

Atonement

The kindling, broken in fistfuls, was arranged
in the center of the stone ring one day when winter
barged into autumn's fading light.

On top of the stones, a small pile of messages
written on rice paper and folded into thumb-sized
packets, each with its own label: Fear, Guilt, Anger.

I squatted and cupped the lit match, succeeding
on the third attempt and with a few soft breaths
on the coals, coaxed the flames to catch.

Righteousness was the first to go, its message
curled and crumpled, the dark ink dissolved to smoke
then drifted a little in the biting breeze.

My disappearing sins warmed me first
before reuniting with everything.

Branch, Drop

Light rain today.
On the maple, drops refuse to fall.
Or is it that the branch won't let go?

All that's needed is to open
the undiscovered room
where the drop — if it fell —
would arrive. And another room —
where the drop will not fall. And another —
before the drop appeared on Earth,
the branch simply being a branch.

Nothing Is Too Wonderful To Be True

The parishioners stood around after church. They poured out
    of the big oak doors and down
the steps. It was spring and warm enough to lean on the banisters
    to talk. Some of the children ran
around. Some hung tight to their parents' coats. No one
    mentioned the sermon. They shared gossip
and recipes and hopes for Bobby, who would pitch later that day.
    Two or three robins hopped
from the new grass to the forsythia and back again. The first
    bumblebee of the season threatened
to upset everyone. Last year the Auxiliary planted some boxwood
    along the granite foundation and
it was here, near the cornerstone, that the gods hid; their books
    opened to the page that defined
chlorophyll and hemoglobin. One molecule's difference:
    magnesium for iron, iron for magnesium.
Of course, this was no surprise to them, being gods, after all. It was
    just one of those little things
that made them laugh.

Triton

Blow on your shell, ancient half-man, grizzled half-fish.
No one will hear you.
Too bad — you're obsolete.

Don't give up, old fellow.
Blow and blow again.
Raise a storm, remind us of our feebleness.
Calm the surf, point out our limitations.

Deliver us from our unbelief.

Learning How To Pray

Learning how to pray means — first of all — unlearning
the ruler-slapped knuckles Sister Mary Marie imposed,

waking myself from Father Phillip's sermons, detaching
all the deeply anchored creeds and catechisms. But,

they are riveted; their elastic tethers snap back
the further they are pulled. These new bruises cover bruises
    barely seen.

Today, sandwiched between two 18-wheelers under the Interstate's
soaring cloverleafs, cheered by the tidy horse farm on the left and
a family mini-van from Spokane, these old words came naturally
    as breath:

Thy kingdom come . . . thy will be done on earth as it is . . .

These are words I was not thinking. These tired words thought
    themselves in me and I,
as if possessed by them, thought: there must be
    a mesh in heaven,

one that drops to earth and weaves itself through me, the highway,
    the waters
and the trees. Some threads are elastic, some withered, others
    newly spun.

There are open places waiting to be filled by my silence and by
what that silence will become.

something for us to stand on

We Know How It Works

We know how it works. The world is no longer mysterious.
—RICHARD SIKEN

Could it be as the poet said?

Flip the switch, the light goes on.
Take the wolves away, the elk eat all the willows.

Yes, the world can be explained.

Someone swallowed the pills.
Someone slept with someone who was not his wife.
One person drew a picture of a bridge, 100 people
climbed the girders with their hammers.

But, when Oppen writes,

knowledge is
loneliness turning and turning,

we know what he means   and we don't know.

How do the cranes find their way home?
Where does a song go after it enters an ear?

The Indian Ocean warms, sand blows in Africa
and the Caribbean stops breathing.
We know it's a matter of one degree
but why don't we stop our burning?

The foghorn reminds us . . . that, even after the perilous crossing,

The self is no mystery. The mystery is
that there is something for us to stand on.

Who understands? Who stands under?
The invisible weight of all that.

We know the number of the gene
but not the day the strand will break.

Life's Second Half

A knowingness: bedrock rising,
softens in contact with the air.

A truth, a teasing
A two-pounder —
wise to the spinner's flash and wiggle.

Monday: potholes
Tuesday: a siren
Wednesday: shoulder shrug
All the others: a long haul from the toilet to the chair.

Tell me, someone:

with the spade of days remaining,
how to turn the soil
and where.

Reliable Equation

An engine rumbles in the brain and is poor
compared to wind or water on the skin.

The heart sets itself with unscheduled thoughts.
No — it is beset with their bright burning.

What remains: scorched boards, smoldering bricks.
The rubble tears at the tenderness there.

I might smell the leafy earth blood beating
while I try to decipher the cold moon.

To think without proof. To feel with certainty.
The wound ever open and warmed by the sun.

Dream

She called out, the way she had so many times before.
"Water. Please. Another pill."

The room this time — darker.
In her regular chair, head hung in the afterlife of mourning.

She cried out, "Everyone told me I would see all the others."
I said it would be soon.

"No. No," her answer, "It will be
a very long time."

I woke trying to picture the room.
Her extra "helping" cushion raises her upright.
Those yellow slippers with the bows.

Each Life Opens

Each life opens when it is ready to open.
And the well fills and the light trickles in.

A gradual process, eventually
the urge to name the growing things disappears.

There's nothing singular. Not the jetty
that swings around the harbor's mouth,
not a dancer's arm across the empty stage.

The pink-purple sunset, the dolphin jumping,
trawlers coming in for the night.
These are words, but not the words for what unfolds
in symphonic hands,
for the ear fine-tuned
to the silence that rises from the well.

Going Without Tea

. . . going without tea holds the hope of tasting it
—Lorine Niedicker

I might believe her if contentment meant
to sip the *thought* of jasmine swirled with sugared milk.

I can't thrive on something bland.

I've stopped to love the untouchable moon,
so thin against the cobalt night.

The dogwood berries are plump and full of red
though before they bloom I'll shake
through 16 weeks of snow and ice.

I can imagine passion and hope for it
the way a furrowed field waits for seed to sink its root.

But no one ever mentioned brittle wind or sand
or locusts after they've devoured all the corn.

At Daybreak, Waiting For The Oriole Under The Serviceberry Tree

I swear — the orange bird *did* come once to this tree under which
    I now sit with my camera and fancy lens. It's good medicine
to wait for a bird, to try to chase it doesn't work. The more I look,
    the faster it recedes, too high into the tall pines. A cardinal came
to rescue me, a ruby throat, too. But they didn't stay long enough
    to do much good.

So, while I contemplate another hard winter passed, the peeled
    paint on the steps I fix each year, a friend — dead, another
pissed off at her boss, and a grandchild yet to arrive, the bees
    in the berry blossoms promise summer pies. And all the while,
the question mark that is the absent oriole whistles the same old
    song. But the bird won't come, has other worms to fry, and
the world won't behave, not even for me, though — by God —
    I wish it would try.

Urine Of Cows Fed On Mango Leaves

Imagine the discovery. Food being scarce, a herder
    gathered the shiny leaves that had fallen
from the single courtyard tree and threw them down
    among the hooves.

The beasts were glad for it, something other than
    scraping for the few tufts left in the dust where
they were staked. And they gorged and chewed,
    chewed and grunted throughout the night.

The next day, the herder — or maybe his children
    passing time among the flies —stepped back
when the first rump arched itself, letting loose its stream.
    And the second and third. Great pools of sunshine

graced the sand and muck. Someone used a stick
    to stir the stuff, someone else scooped it up and
spread it on a leather scrap, just to fool with it, just to
    see what it would become. When the Minister

of Painted Books came to collect his milk, he pinched
    a bit between his finger and his thumb. He gasped
as if the clouded heavens opened for the lighted one.
    The herder and his children became famous in the town.

Priests and artists came for more from miles around.
They planted two more trees and purchased three more cows.

This Evening

This evening there is nowhere to rest but in
the wind. A blue wind comes up through
the floorboards. An orange wind in the gap where
the windows won't meet the sills. These two
winds are complementary and therefore better than
the sofa where I can't sit because one side is empty,
outweighing my wish for someone there.

I Am Not Persian

yet I know all about that thing
Rumi had with Shams.

My way of knowing it
is through argument.

My "somewhere Beloved"
has yet to arrive and my yearning
shows both of us there/not there.

Friendship

Do I know what friendship means?

Like a faraway territory, all-of-a-sudden upon me
and I upon it —

A clearing and a meadow. Oh,
the goldenrod, and another whose silk seeds rustle
then soar in the autumn winds.

There is an absence here so vast.
But close enough to say,
"Here. Here."

I Don't Like People; Animals, Too, Are An Imposition

My neighbor is mean as a chainsaw. Last week he routed
the run-off from his yard to mine. He doesn't give a damn
about his dog, who craps in everyone's garden but his own.
I've tried a friendly nod. Even Christmas pie. I lie in bed at night
wondering if he was damaged as a child. His lover ran off
for another guy. Probably his spleen's enlarged.

I want to treat him as I would myself, but this morning
I lit a paper bag of shit on fire, ran after knocking on his door.
Go ahead: I'm no better than him. I've failed to rise above it
(as my father always said). There's a lesson in here somewhere.
If you can find it, keep it to yourself. I've got chores to do:
chop wood, fix the wall in my yard.

Radio

Candle, clawfoot tub.
A wine glass — half full —
waits on the little table near the door.

Behind the frosted curtain
you are rare,
an orchid in a steamy world.

I stopped — not to gawk
but to record
on Lascaux's modern wall
the melancholy yellow flame,
the pink towel's promise,
your arm's ascent.

After 50,000 years
we have this much left
while the discordant news drones on.

I Have A Softness In Me

I have a softness in me that I want

to be closer to. It lives next to a barbed gatekeeper
who wasn't enlisted.
"Try to pass without bloodshed," it goads.

Yesterday I woke on the right side, unfolded. In too few minutes
I kicked the cat. That's the gatekeeper not letting me out or in.

The Idealist
—for Betsy Boyd

To begin with: eyes like still pools. Clear
like needles, too, going clear through.

A body like a cello's: warm and woody
and lit up with resonance
which means: everything that enters is amplified —
but not until someone pulls the bow; and then,
even the smallest bit of fuzz on a sweater will rise
to what it is: the sales clerk, the stock boy, the trucker,
the packer, the Indonesian weaver in a crowded room,
the hand — gnarled and bumpy — the spinner,
the shearer: that family at the table after chores,
the lamb with its tiny teeth, the clover rooted in the field, the sun.

An idealist is realistic about the scent of an airless room;
the bedpan, the used-up gauze
smell nothing of cinnamon or musk.

And what about memory?
Poland. Birmingham. Aleppo.
An organ to breathe that stuff
and a process of elimination that knits what has happened
into the body, the texture
of thought and of skin,
that half-opened border between self and the world.

And, after sipping cocoa or tea,
the tongue will taste: bittersweet.

The Inner Place Of Finding You

Strangers, adrift
on separate continents,
hone in on the signal: a
belly-spark — and then
embark; each camp packed
and hauled over the pass, each team
tests the echo wall, sends a probe-line
into the crevasse, but deeper than that:
nucleic core
where no one lives.
The Buddhists say: it is
that emptiness.

Tumor

I set the phone in its cradle and watched a warbler
hopping in the autumn dogwood near the gate.

The bird stopped in my yard on its way to Venezuela.
Miniscule. Dusty yellow. Stripe on its wing.

It could sit in my palm, except the little thing is quick
and I'm ashamed of myself for thinking —

in the midst of admiration for the verve inside its hollow bones —
that I could crush it as I could a piece of paper or a leaf.

But it won't be caught and so I'm saved, though not
for any goodness I possess. When my father said

it was on his liver — 10 centimeters by 12, on his liver —
12 seemed too big to be in him, who was big to me

and is big, even now that I am grown. The little warbler
is four inches long. How big is a centimeter?

When I was small he taught me:
to get from inches, we multiply by three.

Stand By Me

On the Number 1 Local, heading uptown on an August night,
I'm shoulder-to-toe with New York's weary workers.
At the far end, a baritone in a linen shirt sings Ben E. King.

The clanky train hollows with his deep song and then, "Give me
a little help, New York," he invites us to join in. I want to sing.
Others do, too. The woman who bobs and sways; she almost
sings. And the one who slides over so I can sit, and the one who
complains with her eyes about being too close to me. But no one does.

"Tough crowd tonight," he laments at 72nd St.
And when he steps out, I feel regret; I need him
more than I thought: *When the night has come,*
and the land is dark, when mountains fall into the sea . . .

Until Now

—for Shay Whitman Cooper

Until now I have not been asked to look
for the rain that is no longer here, the rain —
booming and electric — that pummeled
the blueberries last night, bent the ferns;
that hours before bounced off the stone wall
and into the gravel ditch below the pine. The rain
that by now has become a wavy vapor somewhere near.
And though I consider myself mostly sensitive
to worlds not in front of my nose, and wishing
to impress my new friend with likable aspects of myself,
I couldn't admit my failure when she so delicately asked:
"Do you see last night's rain?"

In "rain years," she's obviously more experienced than me.
I'll bet she can see straight into a raindrop's core
and out again to its gathering source. Until now,
I haven't thought at all about a rain that's passed,
much less that it could be found. Who even thinks
about such things? Maybe a shaman interviewed by a Ph.D.

We drove to the trailhead and, as casually as asking
what I'd like for lunch, she brought me
to where the world is new, washed eternally
in the unfindable and everywhere rain.

Cul-de-sac

How could I have known
way back then —
as I circled the cul-de-sac
on my yellow bike,
that I'd be destined to orbit
a dense hollowness, befriending it
like one might the sound
that returns after
hollering into a well.

Restless

If I were a gardener
I'd make paintings with petals and light.
But I don't know what I am doing.
I uproot plants I should save,
let slugs eat the roses.
I'm restless in a 60-year muddle,
am of this earth but without.

An Agreeable Burden

Two people argue in my dream.
Waking, I ask which part is mine. I am
both of their wanting.

I carry that around all morning.
A heaving backpack.
A satchelful of stars.

What It Must Be Like

Talking to you as if
you could talk to me
from the other end of a can and string.

I'm sure that up there
you are shown to each other as you are:
more light than bone, photons streaming.

Look! That sparrow, ablaze
with what you have added to the sun.

Opening

The mystics say
"to look out is to see in
and to look in is to see out."

I searched the Atlantic horizon for a sign.
What did I find?
An oil tanker, thin plumes of spray,
a few white waves. And the opening
I wish for to the other side.

The Want Fire

The want fire — burning.
Not exactly warm — heatless, even,
but active, neutrinos pushing from within
at the cell's thin wall; they exit in small delight:
eyelash flutter, sigh, tremor at the lips' corner.

We sit, not-quite-touching.
With each exhalation
your breath becomes mine — a delicate fuel,
like a feather windblown and dancing,
free of its body. In its earthliness,
sun-warmed, final. But becoming.
Something else, vital,
impossible to hold.

Quickening

Before the mind clicks into being,
while sleep still domes over us,
our bare legs spoon and slide under flannel and wool.

When you roll toward me, the same quickening
as when the turning season at last warms the soil,
the hard-cased seed aburst in the way-down dark.

First Heat

No such thing as sleep
on this first night of summer heat.

You bring a washcloth wrapped with ice,
and nakedness becomes our only cooling.

To touch too much would undo
the good we've done. Yet,

you lie there, undraped, voicelessly
asking for my hand

to send us both
toward our gathering dream.

How To Say It

The words sink
like a shipwreck, speed
like a bullet.

My friend's brother is dead.

The bitter ones said,
it was his own fault.

His stone heart is a cloud now.

Whose time will come next?
Storm taken.
War taken.
A tiny fracture in a cell.

What are we left with?
The laying out,
the sponge,
a bowl and pitcher.
The stony field
more mineraled than before.

Coming To Terms With It

The white pine near my door is a hub of squawks and chirps.
The great tree's needles bristle in clumps along the branches
and the courting blackbirds gurgle: *O-ka-lay.*

I fled the porch to escape the day, this day that bears down like a fist,
this maw of a day. The undershade is a place to think
about love adrift in the gulf of pride.

Eventually the birds forget the bang the porch door made;
the goldfinch comes back to nibble at a cone; three hooded cowbirds
plot to rob a nest and the doves, who are in love,
top each other with a flap and flutter that dissolve it all into food,
     sex and song.

Williams said there is *not even the unknown for us now*, but, he
     was wrong.
You can't explain regret, and I will grieve for what we had, now lost.
And no one ever has seen *this* waxwing pair pass a hard berry
     between their beaks.

State Of Emergency

Freddie Gray, laid to rest
and the city erupts
under orange haze and chopper blades.

Twitter circulates one young man astride his bike,
gas mask on his face, fist raised against the armored cops.

Churches burn, glass strewn,
vacant homes line the streets, there as they were before.

Behind a couch, crib,
upon a bed, at the table
on the bus, the bike, the train . . .
Somewhere,
love hunkers down.

The Work Of Art
—for Timothy App

The painter arrives, restless and searching
for what cannot be made or held or occupied.

With a heaviness, like Vermeer's pulled-back curtain,
he waits to be astonished by a clarity he hopes for

and by the haze his gesture creates. His effort is our own:
an argument with angles and closed-in spaces,

an attraction to and shying away from their defining lines.
The work does not tell of something seen, but responds

to the call of images held deeply — vessels into which
he pours sky, sea, rain, stone, wind and the dawn's blush;

images a composer might tune to or hear in a dream:
a note, drumbeat, a silence. The way, in childhood, before

walking, before we owned the words "castle" or "gravity,"
we *felt* our way into the tower of blocks, pursued

the riddle of strength and collapse. The work
has heart in it, and emptiness. For that is — after all —

the heart's work: to tell of the dark field's vast cosmos,
the traces left by timeless stars and the danger

of standing before either one for too long. We are grateful
for his patience, his nerve . . . for his thresholds on which

we stand, too — a stage where the twin gods
of loss and perfection draw us further and further in.

Two Pockets

One neighbor, angry about a boundary line,
rips out another's fence.

One of the brothers, neither knows which, cracked the toy.

The eye-witnesses each report their own version; the insurance man
calculates the crumpled fenders on unfavorable terms.

The two spouses are certain about how the rug got stained
when the other forgot to walk the dog.

Three nations share separate ideas about what freedom is,
while candidates and journalists shamblize it all.

It gets worse, and it will get much worse.
The priest tells the abbot tells the imam tells the rabbi tells
the shaman tells the Grand Poobah and the scientist
that the cause is the solution. How can anyone understand?

Look for a "meeting field" in the heart — not the small one that beats
against its cage of ribs. We'll find our solace further in, tucked
in the same vault we use to lock the other out. A larger puzzle waits
for us and, if believed, will put it all to rest:

*Each of us has two pockets. In one is the message; "I am dust and ashes,"
and in the other; "For me the universe was made."*

The Road

There is a road no foot or wheel has traveled on, although
it's rutted with marks made by millions of hearts. Amazing,
the weight of those soft organs.

Back and forth between horizons, back and forth
between gravestones and the stars. Between lips and faces,
breasts and thighs.

A person might stray for a time,
for a good long time. But there's something
about those heart-prints that stays put. We find our way,
can't get lost, no matter how hard we try.

Epithalamion, 45 Years Hence
—for Don and Renee Gorman

It is like the changeable moon: silky-lit and melon-full,
sometimes pocked or sharp as the devil's horns,
sometimes downright dark and not at all.

It is like the tidal sea: one day high and lapping a friendly shore,
the next, crashing at the cliffs
or after that, stranding our little boats in the mud.

Romeo knew without a doubt that Juliet was the sun —
the atomic fire and the source of all that's good
in everything and everyone.

Most of us have searched from shore to shore more than once,
five oceans, seven continents and past the last planet — out
further, even, than the deep field of what can't be seen. Yet,

today, in our very midst, are these twin stars
their reliable orbit: magnetic and shining,
and the best answer we will ever find to love's elusive mystery.

one hundred footsteps

❖

When the dawn bird calls out
to announce the sun's arrival, the moon's
retreat, why does gladness
mix with melancholy like those two
in the sky? Their traces there.

❖

What good are feet when the work
requires thinking? What good is thought when need
scolds and temptation chants:
"Take me, don't take me; give, don't give." There's only
one boat with oars enough to ferry me across.

❖

When the big black bird makes tracks
across the blue-gray sky, I notice
my own tires speeding over
the asphalt; landscape — so quick — disappears.
But deep down that bird stitches lasting shadows for me.

❖

I walk into each day —
a normal way of moving. We all move,
slow down, move again. It's
a parade! But nothing fills me like
the moment of a thumb and finger. Fruit. Skin.

❖

At the moment it's needed,
a raindrop dangles from the pine's tip
where it was lit by the rising sun.
There will be wind or jostle by a bird.
But now, attention — call it prayer.

❖

Pink petals fallen.
In the gutter, in the iron grate, suspended.
A dark river below
will float these fragile boats. When the breeze unmoors
them from their rest place: a flutter and then   gone.

❖

An interruption in
downtown traffic while the crosstown cars
and trucks stream east and west.
So many hearts are breaking, wishes leaping.
Each other's footfalls strike and disappear.

❖

To be born in winter,
to be ice-crunched and hearth-fired, to wish
for land above the tree line.
In the flesh: a dream of sleeping music.
In the bones: a template for cloud breath.

❖

The God of Lost Causes
might laugh at the effort and, too,
the effect of these letters
falling from my hand. Funny: how their curves
and squiggles look like lips and wrinkles as they land.

❖

"Rain is falling. In hushed
silence, rain is falling." Something so moving,
so foreign, in the ancient
mode. A return — though I've never left —
to the harbor's mouth, foghorn, mute light swinging.

❖

We are likely to be surprised
by those who dwell in the other world,
pushing on the paper screen,
a tender membrane. We miss the impression
of their voices and their hands.

like light through the branches

Miracle

Because   from absence
        springs presence.

Because   prior to now
        no story
                and now
                a deer comes slightly forward, but then —
                as if to absorb the immensity of the encounter —
                retreats into the shade.

Miracle means also:
not to shy away from, but to become
awesome, like light through the branches
ushering into existence
each tip of insignificant grass.

What Landscape Paints Itself In Me?

—after Paul Cézanne

I study the lake's light
as it rises pink against blue.

On days with small winds
its face wrinkles; big storms
capsize the shore reeds
and drive the gulls away.

Here, I learn about the collegiality of flocks;
I love the dips and arcs they make.

My own singularity stands out, bone-deep.

Just A Day

Stream crossing, train whistle
among the beech leaves rustling
and a vulture swings down low over the boardwalk
when the engine light barrels over the causeway
and the geese lift over the dormant buds,
ashimmer in the water's mild ripple, in the liquid
where the deer bounding and the dog barking
and the family laughing their way
to the dusk gate closing, though none of us there
were closed or will ever be as long as we remember
what we saw or how it felt to us on that day,
just a day, normal,
a normal day.

An Eagle's Table

Downy feathers swish in the limbs of the small pines.
Loose piles flutter among the needles on the forest floor.

On top of the branchless hemlock, a flat table with tufts
stuck, not flying. A child's curling hair? No,

not lovely. Instead — the site of yesterday's carnage. Or, yes —
lovely — the eagle having had its meal and leaving for us

these gorgeous flags.

Although It's Wasted Now

Although it's wasted now, beached
in the sandy grass, the boat
begins with a spine. Before
the fleet, any weekend pleasure,
a moonish cruise (where kissing happens),
before the Viking's final, fiery trip —
the boat begins. The builder's hand
bends the cypress, molds the metal. And
there are some calculations, an eye-balling
of the curve from bow to stern.
But it's the bony frame that starts it;
the ribs, like fingers, opening after prayer.

Our Lake Is Heart-Shaped

Our lake is heart-shaped and pulsing with lilies, wings and frogs.
When deep into big weather, it froths and tumbles the shoreline
rocks, all the fine tree roots exposed.

Our lake is a teardrop filling from deep springs.
While resting on its surface with sail or paddle,
I am brought beyond my landedness.

Not until diving under can I know its pillowed, dull-moss light:
a soft birthplace of souls where a body is seen at last
for what it is: awash in the eye of God.

Bashō At The Plate: An Ephemeral

—for Thomas Lux

The catcher flings his mask back
and jigs around the plate beneath the foul.

On the next strike, Finnegan is out.
And when Tony cocks back on the mound,
the crowd chants: Moose, Moose,
hoping he'll clock it.

In the frame made
by the catcher's butt
and the umpire's knee,

an April pear tree blooms white
against the green, green field.

Then, after the bat cracks   gone.

How To Paint A Walking Mountain

The puzzle about wisdom is that it makes me dumb. I can't figure
   out what the Zen masters mean: The blue mountains are
   constantly walking.
Or Donovan [remember him?]: First there is a mountain,
then no mountain, then there is. Try telling that to your boss
   on Tuesday.

I can sit all day waiting for that mountain across the lake to
   begin walking.
It's not quite a mountain. Some call it a knob; others, a rise. But
   from where
I sit, Morse Hill is the horizon's highest point and is mountain-
   like enough.

If I were a painter, I'd use some blue, though mostly gray or
   hunter's green.
Rilke on Cézanne would confirm that I'd need all three to get the
   color of the mountain today.

In any case, I can sit all day waiting for that hill to start walking.
   I've checked
on it while chopping wood. And except for its reflection swirling
   on the lake's
surface, I can tell you — that chunk of hemlock, oak and granite
   is going
nowhere, has planted itself in place where the lake becomes a
   river on the other side of the dam.

I can plop myself in my chair with a notebook and boxful of colors.
I can try to describe that place. And soon enough it becomes a
   friend — up close,

in bed or across the table. The place has more folds and canyons
than can ever be

seen or even imagined. Hawks in the pines, red fox darting into
the ravines and

centipedes under the rotted log; a purple hat hangs on a limb
where the creek

pools up enough for a body to bend down to have a drink.

That's the thing about mountains, about looking. There's always
more. If we

were to walk up the Shutesbury Road and over the old stone dam,
we'd pass

a divot in the road; one of us would trip on the bumpy surface
and, in falling,

would spot a moss-trail obscured by the laurels. We'd see that it
leads to an old

graveyard, lush with blueberries for the taking. And though
there's some

disrespect in that, we'd probably eat a few, which is like eating
the mountain,

at least the blue part. I need practice in unflattening what my
eye sees.

The neighbors say a fisher cat lives back in those woods. And,
while we are

supposed to love all wild things, the books say they will — like
any good demon —

bite you in the face. So, there's no way in hell I'm going to verify
what goes on over there at night.

Harvest, Hatfield, Massachusetts

On the left side of a two-lane country road,
a man on a tractor pulls a rack of tobacco leaves.

It's the hottest summer anyone remembers: dust 90-plus degrees.
He digs deep for an ear of corn —

two creamy kernels stuck to his chin — then turns off the macadam
onto a dirt road that stretches toward a river somewhere.

We watch his trail rise over the vast collage of half-eaten fields;
the workers' shirts, a celebration of orange and green.

We stop to take a picture. Diesel heat. The tractor's rattle.
Rows and rows of heart-shaped poisonous leaves.

Treasure

Pumpkinseed. Or bluegill, maybe. But maybe not,
because of those orange marks; its gill flap has a red spot.

Sunshine gilts the clear lake water and shafts
clean through to the bottom sand,
ground by ice and waves from granite chunks,
but now a gold-glittered stage
for yellow perch, blacknose shiners,
and all the silvery minnows zip, zipping.
And the pumpkinseed or bluegill
waving its common tail to me —
belly down on this wooden dock. And pocketless.

Axis Mundi

In the hemlock forest
on an old lumberman's road,

the end of light. Last leaves falling.

The trees, their skeletal shapes.
And on the road, a creature
too far to fully see.

And so we stopped,

and all the sounds stopped,

and the animal kept walking.

And so we made,
on the long road,
a kind of axis:

the creature and the people.

And in the vibration between these poles:

All that we are and all we are not.

On either side of the road:
the uncultivated forest, all its wild distance.

And then a crow, flying low,
issued its warning.

And the bobcat,
which had, by this time, come close to us,
saw the danger there
and then was gone.

Wayfinding

Winter falls from the sky and bends
the hemlock branches. They kneel
to touch the ground.

Snow: heaven come to earth.
Footsteps, like owl wings,
soft on the roadless road.

My imprint disappears
as soon as its mark is made.

Hammerhead

Sundrenched, the benevolent Gulf lies flat and aquamarine.
Our rented boat chugs offshore from Three Rooker Key,
and the pelicans, looking Jurassic, dive for mullet.
The shrimp bucket slip-sloshes under our feet.

A great day to fish. Except, I don't like the thought of catching them.
But you do. And I like watching you: bait the hook, cast the rod,
and the hard power of your curse when things don't work.

The clever fish eat the shrimp right off the hook.
"We're feeding *them*," I say.
"That's not helpful," you say back.
And the timing couldn't be better because just then
your rod tip dips way down

and you play it a little to be sure it's caught. The line pulls taut,
producing the promising arc of the bent-over rod.
Something flashes in the water, zig-zags toward the boat.
Hammerhead! An infant, 2-feet long, and the hook
sunk clear through its lip. A wild thing on our boat bottom,
choking in the paradoxical light.

It was my job, you said, to get the hook out, the hook
that pierced clear through its toothy lip, the hook
with a ring of red now growing on the alabaster skin.

I was glad to have a task and, like a pro,
pressed my foot against its spine, behind the signature fin.
The young shark's life pinned under my shoe's rubber tread.
The damn cutters, rusted dull, wouldn't clip the hook

and the air grew fast with dying.
I said, "The only way is to pull the hook out backwards."
It was easy and slid through the lip with a soft *pop*.

I slid it to the water quick,
releasing its elegant tail from my fleshy hand.
It swam straight down leaving us alone
with the crests of the glittery waves.

What Do You Think

What do you think of the little egret
tip-toeing through the marsh?
White feathers ruffed against
the slate-blue Gulf.

See how it lifts its foot,
like a Chinese painter who lifts her brush.

Having Arrived On The Other Side

I lift a shell from under the Verrazano's miraculous span.
Granite sands glitter my hand and —
for a moment — I feel like Blake,
even though I'm worlds apart
from the oyster becoming light in a sea gull's gut,
from the source of the shell's pearl-sheen in the late summer sun.

Far from Brooklyn, I'm on the Narrow's other side.
having left from there, muffled
and now here, with a mollusked heart.

Her Good Hat

—for Sandra Connors

My neighbor wears her old green hat
when she is in her boat. The cotton
sags with 40 years of wind and wave;
the brim's too thin for shade; no strap
to hold it snug. She's the only one
who knows: the hat is good because
it tunes her to the lake, to herself.
Together they dip the paddle
into deep water, glide toward the cove.
Like fin and scale,
feather and hollow bone.

Becoming

—for Elliott Barker

The wind blows hard and I'm in a rush
to make the little boat right.

An experienced know-it-all, I've read
in my books about jib and jibe.

Many times I've muscled my way or failed
to come well-enough about. Today,

I crashed full speed into the dock.
The lesson I am learning

is that the blue lake deepens
as the gusts approach; blue

becomes bluer, stripes of darker blue
edge the wavelet crests. I listen, now,

to the tiller's hum in my hand.
I have what I need to become

the long-winged heron
that does not struggle to land.

Intimate Distance

A white-haired lady in a pink shirt
picks her way among the rocks.

Spartina — a field of it — leans
toward a sliver of hard sand.

The water is wave-rich today. Spinnakers
and tugs move on it
and people, who jump and dip.

From a distance they are a pointillist's dream
urging me to strip, slip
into a sea so heavy with blue
it sticks to my skin.

As intimate as the pink wrapping her shoulders.

To feel that close to her.

New England Graveyard Under Snow

The sky falls soft for two days straight
and muffles all the tombs. Drifts cover
the poorer folk, erasing almost everyone,
except for Fiske and Mrs. Wirth,
both rich enough to afford the tallest stones.

The souls residing here must know —
better than collectors of Currier & Ives —
the rustic hominess of rough-hewn gates,
the granite vault and the newly planted rugged cross.
They huddle now, without their names, without
their dates, among the roots, against the unforgiving cold.

I trudge a path to tilted, nearly buried markers,
although I'm not sure why. To be among them,
practicing — my own passing not far behind,
my generation's "age of optimism"— gone.

It's hard to think of a world without me in it.
The movies I love will go on. My children, my children's
children. A color — gorgeous in a painting or in the sky.
Celestial gases and fires, hard particles of asteroids.
And meanings — that singular game I play while alive —
will collide with those that the living adopt and memorialize.

To the neighbors passing in their cars, I must be
a disruption to death's privacy. I avert and apologize.

Back at home, with my photographs and few poetic lines —
How else should I respond? For the time being — alive.

Cityscape

Rat trap row houses glitter in the setting sun.
We are alive! Hauling our heavy loads
home from the hard work of body and of mind.

The weak roses among the bricks on Clement Street
are cared for in the gravel bed at the alley's edge.
A purple flamingo and the smaller pink one
nest in a cactus pot, wings clattering
in the harbor's wind.

The working hulks at the dock's edge
open their monumental arms
to unload steel boxes filled with junk and cars.

From high in the lifeboat, a stevedore
plays his bagpipes as the sun goes down
and the evening fills with *Amazing Grace*,
lighting us, every single one.

The Bird Artist

Chagrined with the damage his hands laid to the page,
the bird artist wrote in a letter:

"They are all far below
the little pictures I have in my mind."

I, too, have a picture: Texas hills. A flash in the mesquite.
Your bootsteps on the path as you come close

to help me match the creature
with the drawings in our book.

The difficulty of naming it — the bird, yes;
but also your breath. No word for that scent,

filled with flying and deeply hued,
though unpaintable.

First Walk

The two birds flew behind us and one circled back for you.
I was sure it was an eagle, wishing — as I do always —
for a more majestic world.
We can want that, can't we? A life
made larger by what we hope for? Like the possibility
that strangers will arrive where they need to be so they can meet.

When we walked under the Spanish moss after ten years of winter
and you sat next to me on the log in the sun,
unmistakably the little night heron's gray-blue
blended perfectly with the bayou's sheen.
A wind from the Gulf glazed the live oak's leaves.
A stand of palmettos announced our awkwardness
with the clatter of their fans.

Aubade

I love the generous moon in earliest daylight.
Full, not yet falling, it hangs
above the hillside's spruce.

Between us, a rose-dawn
colors the grass blades.
My lovely moon.
My heartbeat
reaches further out, further in. And just now,
geese rising from behind the ridgeline
soar over me.

Prayer

I will build a boat of mud and wattle,
lined with grass and moss. In it I'll wrap
the troubles of the ones I love
and all the wrongs I've done.

On a night when the full moon's gentle light
frosts a path offshore,
I'll give the boat a little shove, hope
it won't capsize on the shoals.

Off you go, mild vessel,
be steadfast in the wind.
Your cargo needs a resting place.
Lord, keep it safe amidst the rocks and dorsal fins.

Readiness

Breathing begins with a walk across the boatyard:
oil-soaked gravel, cradled hulls.

Each of these is a heartbeat: step
down, into the wooden dinghy; set
two leather-wrapped oars in brass sockets.

A yellow-eyed gull dips over the green marsh.
Our little black boat rests close across the river: cleats,
coiled cotton ropes, tea and pillows in the cabin,
five sails stowed below.

Becoming An Impressionist

—for Mary Cornish

The sky flutters with color.
Pink petals like snowflakes falling. It's spring
and the one I love wears lavender on Sunday.

Unleashed in a dandelion field,
a dog spurs 12 yellow butterflies,
like blossoms, loose from their roots.
And I scratch my head, hoping you'll see them,
little metaphors, like Monet
who hoped to paint — not the boats and houses —
but the air in which he found them.

Sunshine washes the grass,
each candle blade wet with light.
A blue-black bug with angel wings
rubs its wiry arms
then clings to a stem that bends as I walk by.

Like Rilke, to see and be seen. This
unequivocal light. This life.

3 The book's title, *Almost Entirely*, comes from a Hayden Carruth poem, "Testament," which is also referred to in "Carruth"

5 The epigraph contains a quote from the preface of Jorge Luis Borges's *Labyrinth: Selected Stories and Other Writings*.

15 The ending lines of "When the Wing Gives Way" are inspired by Christian Wiman.

16 Italicized lines in "And God Goes Blank" are from *A Poet's Bible*, by David Rosenberg.

18 "Thamar dreamt of birds in her throat" is from Federico García Lorca's poem "Thamar and Ammon." The Roman Catholic ritual "Blessing of the Throats" celebrates the feast day of Saint Blaise.

20 "The wind of God moved over the face of the waters" is from Genesis 1:2.

21 "Requiem" follows (loosely) the seven-part Roman Catholic funeral mass. "The rope that holds until we need it" is from C. S. Lewis's *A Grief Observed*. "The nothingness that is not God" is from Thomas Merton. Thanks to Garrett Crabb for his thoughts about the afterlife as "a collection of broken hours." "Our cup of shadow overflowing" is from Antonio Machado's poem "Siesta." Azure, in the section entitled "Deliver Them," refers to a small butterfly by the same name. A "death planted in us so deeply" alludes to ideas contained in Rilke's *Book of Hours*. "Restless until we rest" is from St. Augustine.

33 Italicized lines in "We Know How it Works" are from George Oppen's poems "World, World—." The poem's title is from Richard Siken's poem "Dirty Valentine."

40 "Urine Of Cows Fed On Mango Leaves" is an imagining of the origin of the pigment Indian yellow, used in illuminated manuscripts.

50 "Stand By Me" refers to the 1961 Ben E. King song by the same name. Reprinted by permission of Hal Leonard LLC.

61 "Coming To Terms With It" contains a line from William Carlos Williams's poem "The Woodpecker."

63 "The Work Of Art" reflects on the 2013 retrospective exhibition of painter Timothy App.

64 "Two Pockets" refers to a rabbinical story told by Joan Chittister in her book *Living in the Breath of the Spirit — Reflections on Prayer.*

67 *One Hundred Footsteps* — The poems here are excerpted from a limited edition artist book collaboration with Katherine Kavanaugh, containing 50 letterpress-printed poems and 50 collaged images printed on rice paper. The project was inspired by the renga, a medieval Japanese collaborative form.

71 The first two lines from "Rain is falling" are from a poem by Tatsuji Miyoshi.

82 "How To Paint A Walking Mountain": "The blue mountains are constantly walking," from Ta-Yang Shan K'ai [in John Daido Loori's *The Eight Gates of Zen: a Program of Zen Training,* Boulder, CO: Shambala Publications, 2002.]

97 "The Bird Artist" took its initial inspiration from the letters of George Sutton and Louis Fuertes Agassiz.

Grateful acknowledgment is made to the following journals in which poems, sometimes in slightly different forms, are forthcoming or first appeared.

America	"Just a Day," "The Wind of God "When the Wing Gives Way"
Arts	"Until Now"
Barrow Street	"Life's Second Half"
Coal Hill Review	"How To Say It"
Georgetown Review	"Quickening"
Literature and Belief	"Opening" & "Wayfinding"
Penwood Review	"The Landscape Paints itself in me"
River Oak Review	"The Bird Artist"
Spiritus	"Reliable Equation" & "And God Goes Blank"
The Innisfree Poetry Journal	"What it Must be Like" & "Restless"
The Worcester Review	"Harvest, Hatfield, Massachusetts"
Zone 3	"Axis Mundi" & "Miracle"

"Branch, Drop," "Tumor," "Requiem," "Radio," "First Walk," "Becoming an Impressionist" appeared in the anthologies *Desire Path* (Chappaqua, NY: Toadlily Press, 2005), *Poetry in Medicine: An Anthology of Poems about Doctors, Patients, Illness and Healing* (New York: Persea Books, 2015) and *Beloved On Earth: 150 Poems of Grief and Gratitude* (Dulmuth, MN: Holy Cow! Press, 2009). "The Work of Art" appeared in a retrospective exhibition catalog, *Timothy App: The Aesthetics of Precision, Forty-five Years of Painting*, Goya Contemporary, 2013.

The following poems were published in *The Want Fire* (Baltimore: Passager Books, 2015): "What do you Think," "Cul-de-sac," "Restless," "An Agreeable Burden," "At Daybreak…," "What it Must be Like," "Having Arrived on the Other Side," "Just a Day," "Opening," "Bashō at the Plate," "Her Good Hat," "Second Half," "Harvest," "Quickening," "First Heat," "Becoming," "Want Fire," "Intimate Distance," "The Bird Artist," "Atonement," "This Evening," "How to Say It," "Aubade," "Readiness," "Wayfinding."

Many thanks to all those friends and family who provide inspiration and support: Anna Catone, Victoria Givotovsky, Michael Salcman, Allen Strous; and especially Judy Remmel. My beautiful sons, Brian and Daniel—you are with me always.

ABOUT THE AUTHOR

Jennifer Wallace lives in Baltimore, Maryland, and in Shutesbury, Massachusetts. She teaches at the Maryland Institute College of Art. Her poetry collections include a chapbook, *Minor Heaven* (Chappaqua, NY: Toadlily Press, 2005), *It Can be Solved by Walking* (Baltimore: CityLit Press, 2012) and *The Want Fire* (Baltimore: Passager Books, 2015). Her poems, essays and photographs have appeared in artists books, exhibition catalogs, galleries, museums, anthologies and literary journals. She edits poetry for *The Cortland Review*.

ABOUT PARACLETE PRESS

Who We Are

Paraclete Press is a publisher of books, recordings, and DVDs on Christian spirituality. Our publishing represents a full expression of Christian belief and practice—from Catholic to Evangelical, from Protestant to Orthodox.

We are the publishing arm of the Community of Jesus, an ecumenical monastic community in the Benedictine tradition. As such, we are uniquely positioned in the marketplace without connection to a large corporation and with informal relationships to many branches and denominations of faith.

What We Are Doing

PARACLETE PRESS BOOKS | Paraclete publishes books that show the richness and depth of what it means to be Christian. Although Benedictine spirituality is at the heart of who we are and all that we do, we publish books that reflect the Christian experience across many cultures, time periods, and houses of worship. We publish books that nourish the vibrant life of the church and its people.

We have several different series, including the bestselling Paraclete Essentials and Paraclete Giants series of classic texts in contemporary English; Voices from the Monastery—men and women monastics writing about living a spiritual life today; our award-winning Paraclete Poetry series as well as the Mount Tabor Books on the arts; bestselling gift books for children on the occasions of baptism and first communion; and the Active Prayer Series that brings creativity and liveliness to any life of prayer.

MOUNT TABOR BOOKS | Paraclete's newest series, Mount Tabor Books, focuses on the arts and literature as well as liturgical worship and spirituality, and was created in conjunction with the Mount Tabor Ecumenical Centre for Art and Spirituality in Barga, Italy.

PARACLETE RECORDINGS | From Gregorian chant to contemporary American choral works, our recordings celebrate the best of sacred choral music composed through the centuries that create a space for heaven and earth to intersect. Paraclete Recordings is the record label representing the internationally acclaimed choir Gloriæ Dei Cantores, praised for their "rapt and fathomless spiritual intensity" by *American Record Guide;* the Gloriæ Dei Cantores Schola, specializing in the study and performance of Gregorian chant; and the other instrumental artists of the Arts Empowering Life Foundation.

Paraclete Press is also privileged to be the exclusive North American distributor of the recordings of the Monastic Choir of St. Peter's Abbey in Solesmes, France, long considered to be a leading authority on Gregorian chant.

PARACLETE VIDEO | Our DVDs offer spiritual help, healing, and biblical guidance for a broad range of life issues including grief and loss, marriage, forgiveness, facing death, bullying, addictions, Alzheimer's, and spiritual formation.

Learn more about us at our website:
www.paracletepress.com or phone us
toll-free at 1.800.451.5006

SCAN
TO
READ
MORE

Paraclete Poetry Anthology

ISBN: 978-1-61261-906-4
$20.00 French flaps

This anthology spans the first ten years of the poetry series at Paraclete Press. Included are poems by Phyllis Tickle, Scott Cairns, Paul Mariani, Anna Kamieńska, Fr. John-Julian, SAID, Bonnie Thurston, Greg Miller, William Woolfitt, Rami Shapiro, Thomas Lynch, Paul Quenon, and Rainer Maria Rilke.

"Paraclete is a house firmly rooted in presenting and curating religious poetry as part of the verbal experience that, being couched more deeply in the aesthetic than the didactic, has deep resonance and potent significance for the shaping of the surrounding culture itself. It means the on-going giving away and sharing of God with humility through mystery." — PHYLLIS TICKLE (1934–2015)

Still Pilgrim

Angela Alaimo O'Donnell
ISBN: 978-1-61261-864-7
$18.00

Still Pilgrim is a collection of poems that chronicles the universal journey of life as seen through the eyes of a keenly observant friend and fellow traveler. The reader accompanies the Still Pilgrim as she navigates the experiences that constitute her private history yet also serve to remind us of our own moments of enlightenment, epiphany, and encounter with mystery. Each of the 58 poems of the collection marks a way station along the pilgrimage, a kind of holy well where the Pilgrim and reader might stop and draw knowledge, solace, joy, and the strength to continue along the path.

Available from your local bookseller or through Paraclete Press:
www.paracletepress.com; 1-800-451-5006